What We Have in Common

A Brim Coloring Book

Written by Jane Landey
Edited by David Austin
Drawings by David Austin and Jane Austin

Published by CreateSpace: An Amazon Company.
Printed in U.S.A.

Introduction

What We Have in Common. Brim coloring books display the similarities of related animals. In this series the pig and the tapir are compared. The facts enable children to appreciate common values. Thus, imbibing in them an interest towards animals which could make them appreciate what they have in common with one another.

The Pig

And

The Tapir

The Pig and the Tapir have many things in common.
They look alike and snout with their noses.
Pig lives with people while Tapir lives in the forest.

The pig and the tapir meet on a refuse dump.

I am a pig.

I am a tapir.

I have a long mouth!

So do I!

I have a snout!

I have a snout too!

My skin is thick.

My skin is thick too.

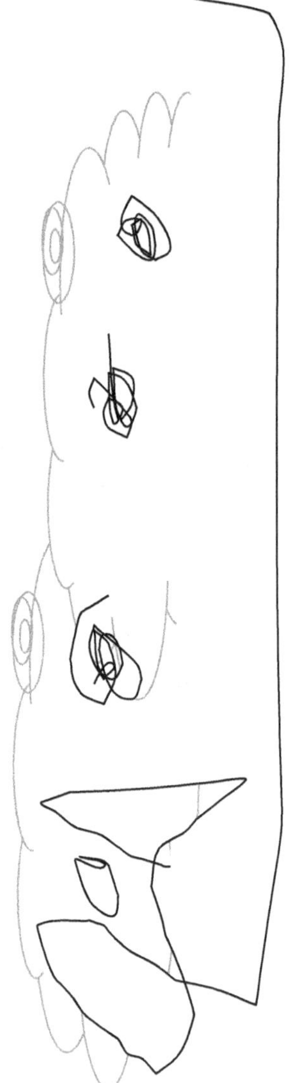

I snout for food.

I snout for food too!

My ears flop.

My ears can flop too!

And I can run.

And I can run too!

My tail is short.

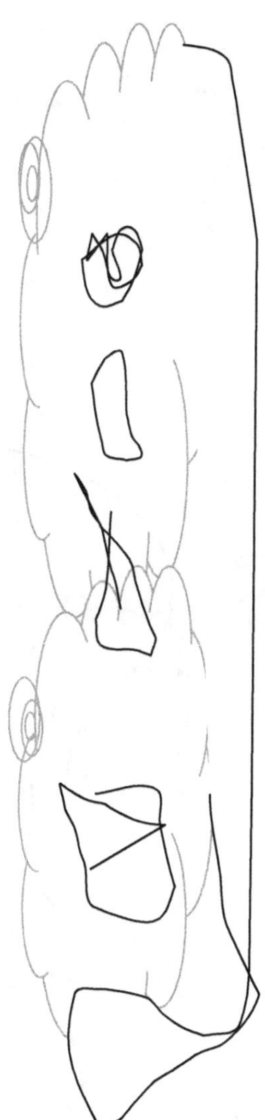

I have a short tail too!

My snout let me look for food.

Me too! Let us look for food.

Alright! I can see some yummy
around here!

Really? We can snout for yummy
yummy now!

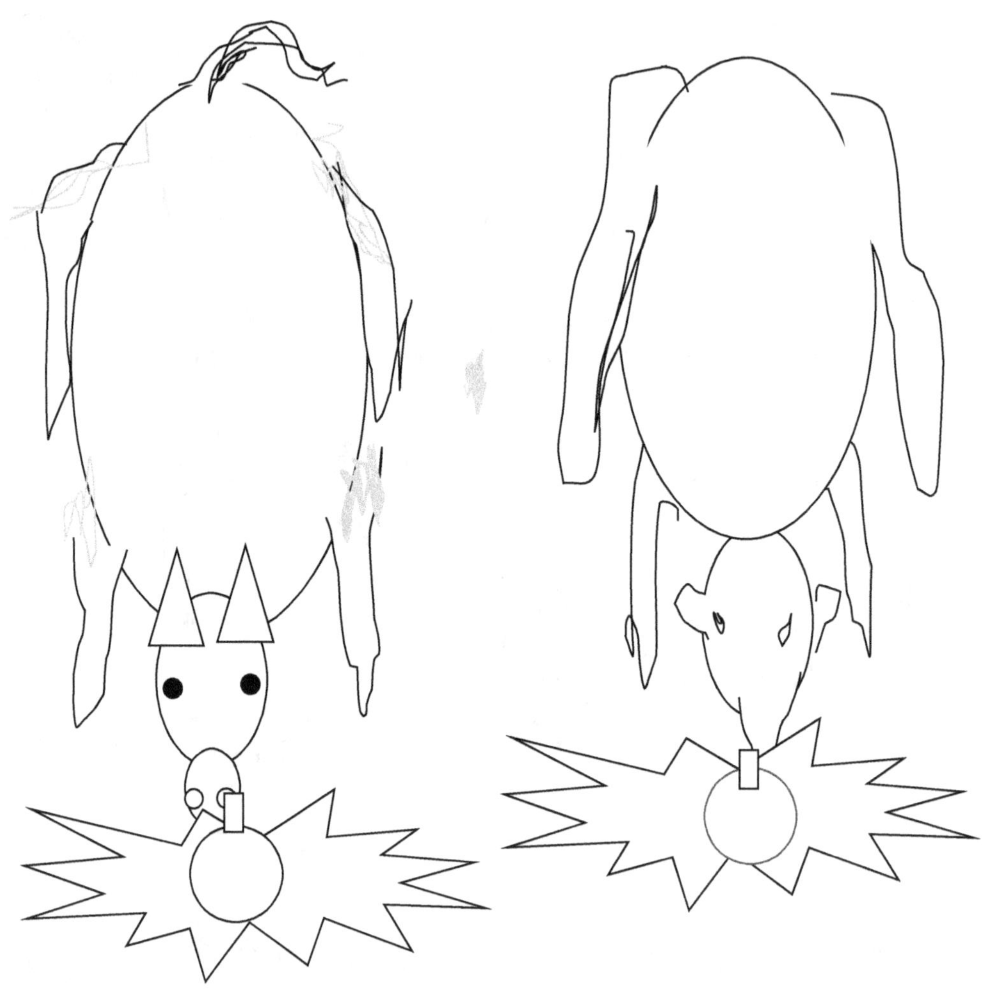

This is an apple.

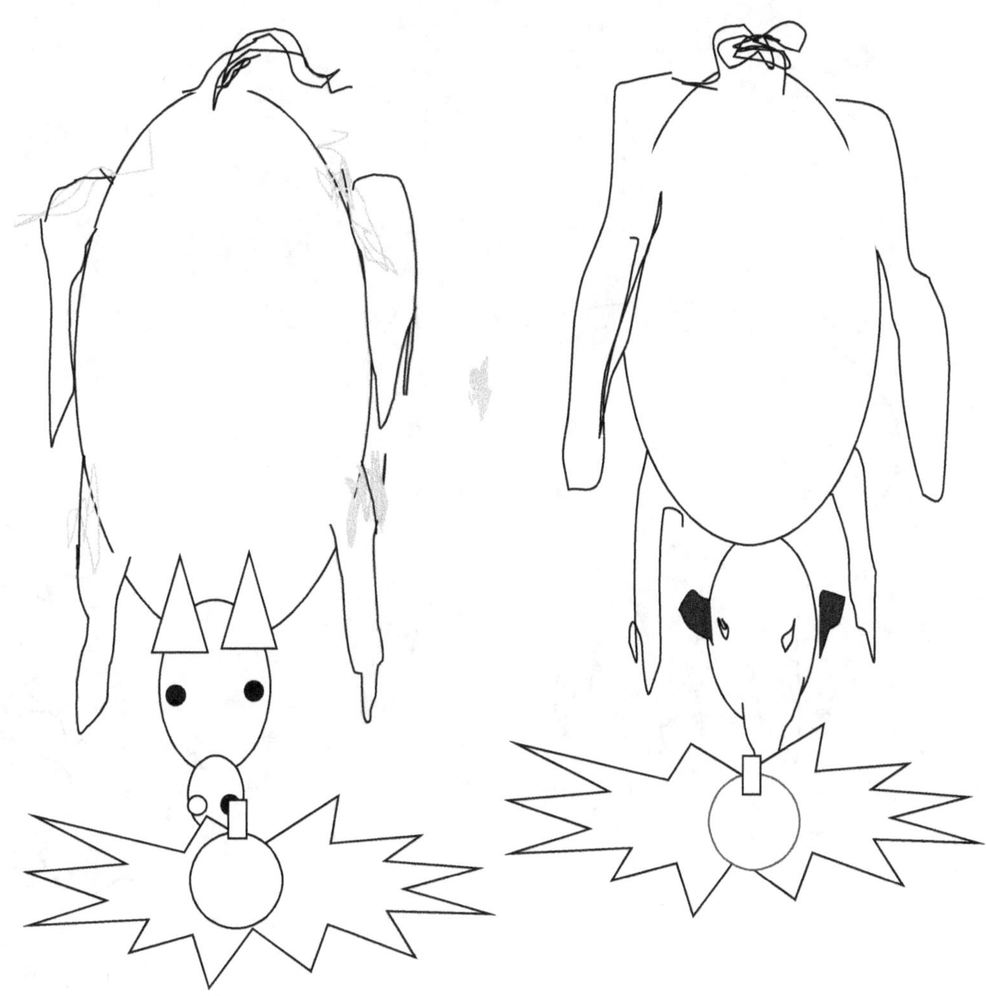

I love to eat apple too.

I can see oranges over there.

Do you like oranges?

Yes I do!

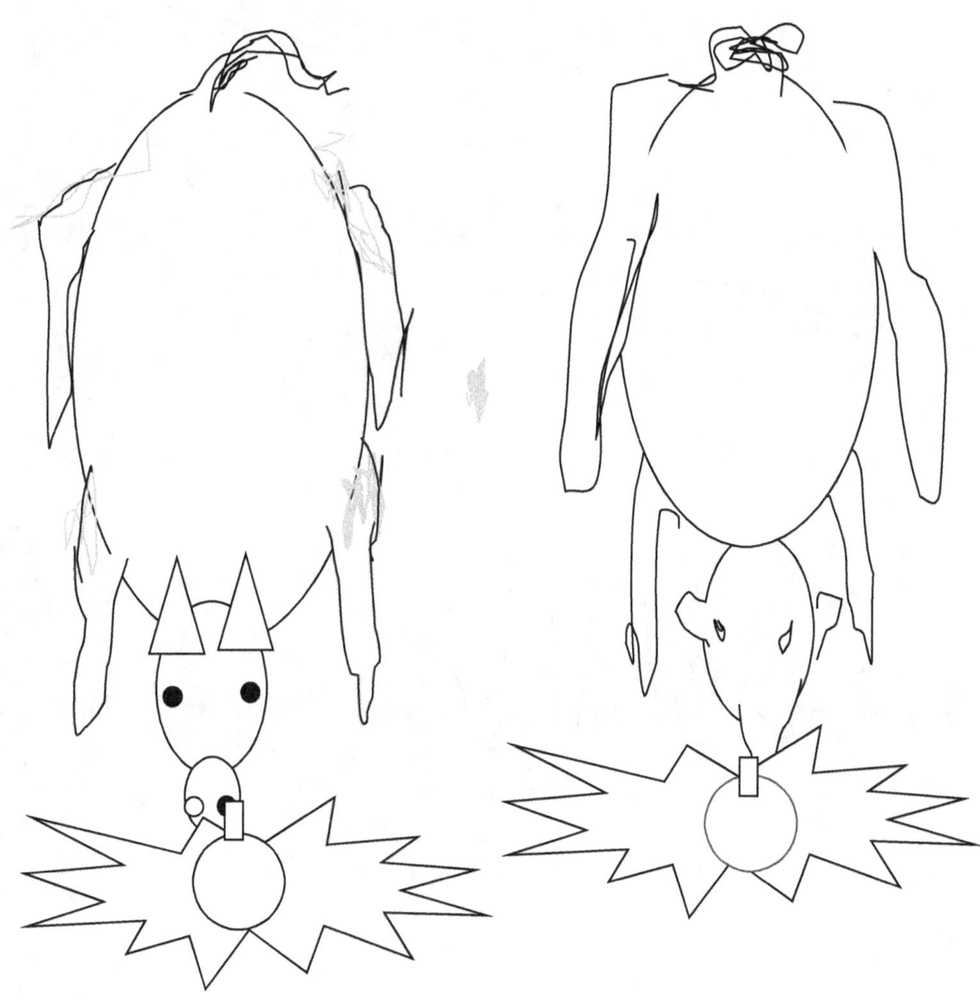

Here, take it and eat it.

What else can you find?

Let me look.

Anything?

Come over! Come over!

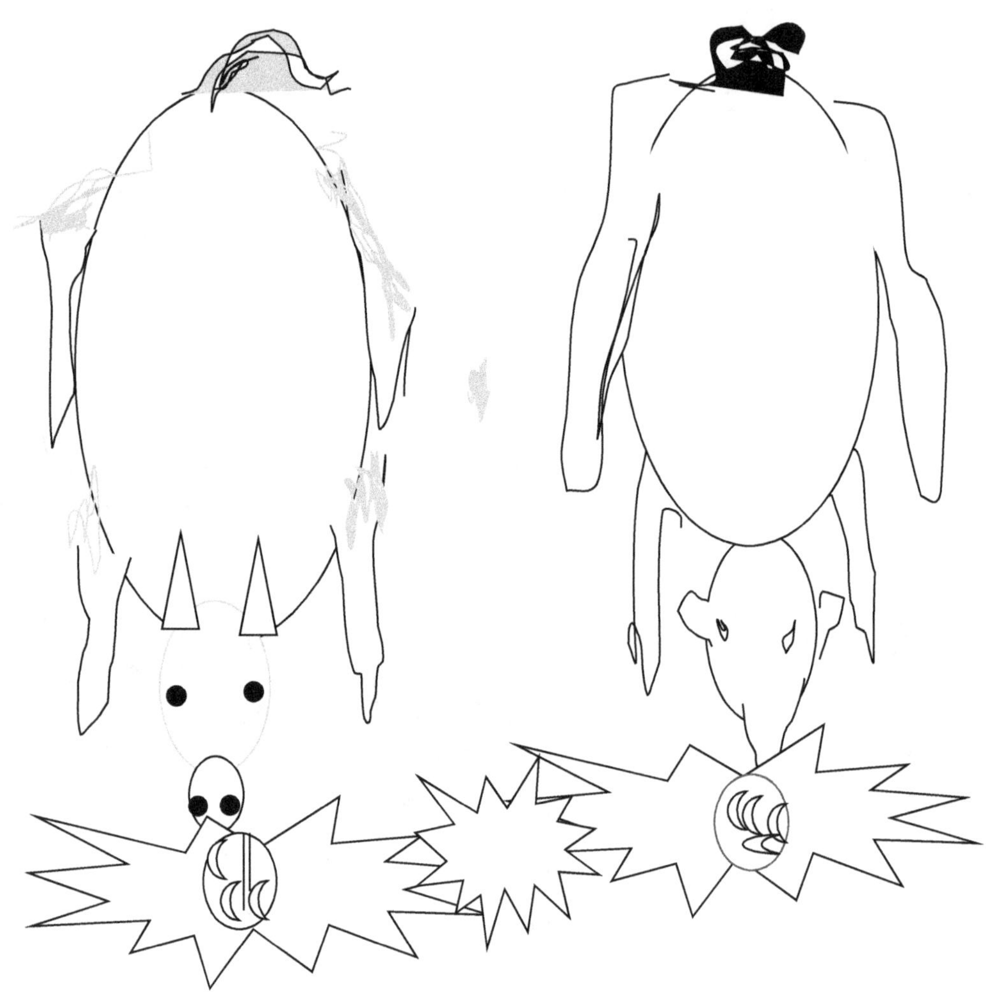

Hmmm ..... yummy, yummy sweet
watermelon!

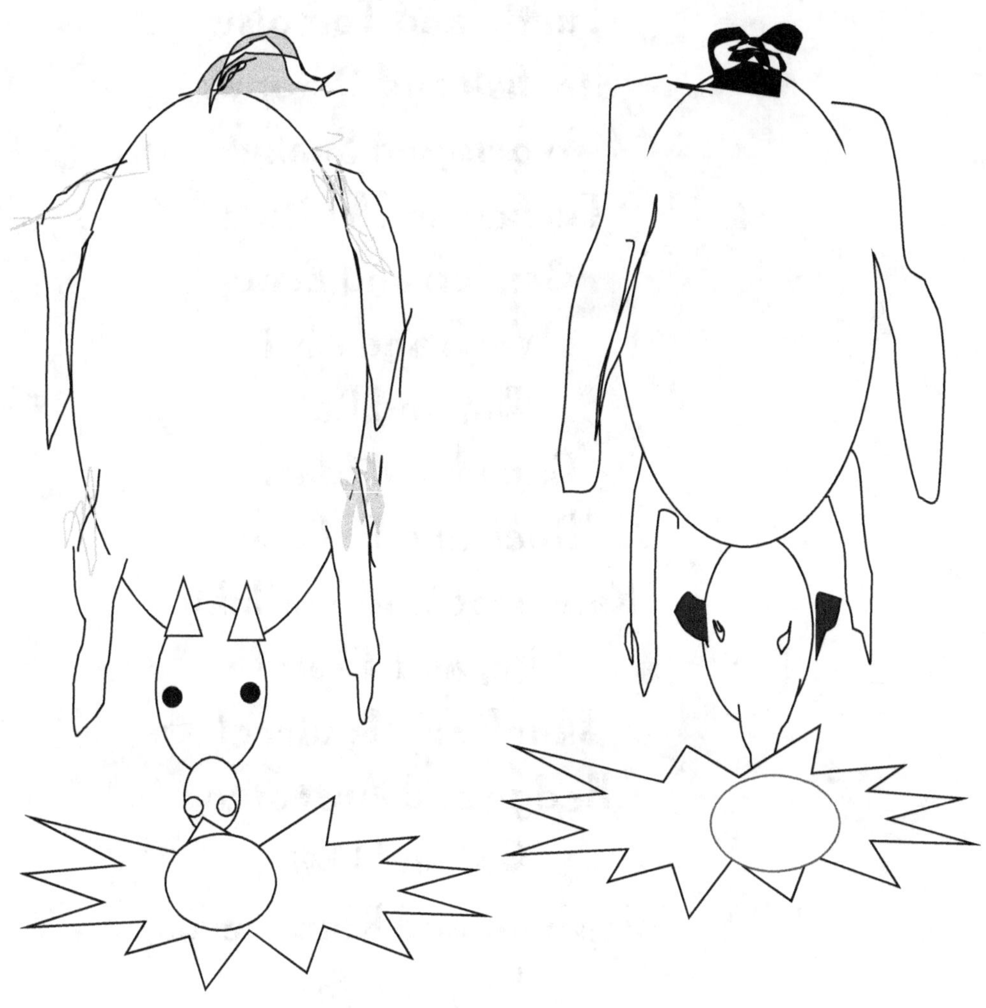

We can eat these together!

What We Have in Common Brim Coloring Books

Crocodile and Alligator
Turtle and Tortoise
Starfish and Octopus
Worm and Snake
Turkey and Vulture
Ostrich and Emu
Weka and Kiwi
Bat and Rat
Camel and Llama
Duck and Pelican
Kangaroo and Wallaby
Pig and Tapir
Skunk and Squirrel
Hedge and Anteater
Cat and Owl
Elephant and Rhinoceros
Dog and Fox
Buffalo and Bull
Leopard and Cheetah
Horse and Zebra